MICHAEL DAABOUL

The
SPACE TIME
FILLED

VOLUME 1

Published by Michael Daaboul

First published in 2020

Copyright © Michael Daaboul 2020

www.michaeldaaboul.com

facebook.com/michaeldaaboul
Instagram @_michaeldaaboul
Twitter @michaeldaaboul

ISBN 978-0-6489069-0-2 (paperback)

NATIONAL
LIBRARY
OF AUSTRALIA

A catalogue record for this
work is available from the
National Library of Australia

For Murphie,
our sea warrior.

This book will hold you when you are crying
because it understands that you are a miracle.

You carry emotions for the world to see,
to climb mountains in search of love and resilience.

This journey will be painful, but it will show you
a life where the core is sweet and ripen
for healing.

Contents

Introduction

1   Genesis   1

2   Sunset   61

3   Sunrise   137

    Terminus   205

    Acknowledgements   215

    About the Author   219

    Index   221

INTRODUCTION

The Space Time Filled: Volume 1 was slow to complete because the endpoint was unimaginable. So I continued to write, undecided of when to stop and the book's direction was vague until the gruelling final edits.

Life is comparable to this book. You keep going, but the destination is a mystery, and breaking the codes where these secrets live could be an eternal struggle. Yet, our curiosity takes us to places where dreams would envy. Life is intelligent and precise but saturated with uncertainty.

The poetry and prose in this collection leap into these unknowns. To give you hope and try to find the answers, whatever secrets and meaning you are looking for inside your heart.

Ever since I could look up, I have admired the Universe. Witnessing the light emitted by the stars upon a pitch-black canvas is an awe-inspiring sight. The mysteries of interstellar space are waiting, but we are prisoners under a beautiful blue sky and a night full of promise.

I wanted to capture emotions in this volume because feelings can transcend the barrier keeping us from figuring out the bigger questions.

Humanity has changed, but our emotions have not moved. We are familiar with love, loss, hurt and healing. They live within, dancing in one transient chaos, and falling on its head as we ponder in nostalgia.

When I lost my first child Murphie, it locked my partner and me inside a void, a black hole where nothing but time filled the darkness. We stayed in torment long enough until we became numb to continue living our lives because the world turned without us. The title originates from this helplessness.

Our hearts broke and exploded into a million fragments. The emotions became overwhelming, taking up room in our minds and settling inside our stomachs. The shattered pieces gave us lessons that we would have never known until they cut us. What lived underneath the surface was terrifying.

By suppressing emotions, it could impede the rebuilding process if we ignored them. If you hide from the suffering, emotions may manifest and bleed into other areas of your life. These feelings could kill you if you are not strong enough to listen to what they are trying to tell you. Listening is critical because when you break, it is challenging to live and all you do is dwell in the ever-growing space that does not stop expanding.

You are powerless to control the pain. We pretend that it does not exist and turn to distraction to find peace for the rest of our lives. Humans will live through suffering, and the poetry will break down the coming of pain, the hurt and the healing. The recovery is hard, but this book is with you.

This collection has three chapters. The first, "Genesis" is the journey through the birth of life where we are learning to understand and survive the struggle of raw emotions. The second, "Sunset," where we find ourselves lost in the darkness, in fear and vulnerable to everything we have to face. The third, "Sunrise," forms the overarching narrative to fight what we endure—searching for hope and happiness.

I hope you discover something special within these pages that you can take with you. I believe this book is the light you need.

We are figuring out this life as one.

Welcome to *The Space Time Filled: Volume 1*, it has been eager to meet you.

The Space Time Filled: Volume 1

CHAPTER 1

GENESIS

There is always a beginning.

It starts with darkness
because you cannot see
if you will make it.
You do not feel pain at this moment.
You are in complete bliss.

If you are part of the lucky ones,
you will be born.
You will start to see,
begin to feel,
and experience another world.
It is the start of happiness,
the beginning of sadness,
and the start of everything
that will come to hurt you.

It is where it all began
before the end.

Genesis

A Heaven You Never Knew

A mother carries you
for nine months,
and then
   you are born.
Before that,
your mother was
your entire universe.

Jubilant

There are stars sprinkled across her eyes,
   and when she left,
I looked towards the night sky
hoping to find her
   on top of the world.

Touching Love

It all starts
with the touch
of her lips.

Unconditional Love

She does not know you,
but she is waiting to see
what you look like,
    what it feels like,
to have you look
into her eyes.

She has not met you before,
but you will be
the love of her life.

Song and Dance

Hold my body
and pull my strings,
play me right,
and I will sing.

Jump into the Abyss

I will show you
> how to love me
if you follow my hands
inside the darkest parts
of me.

Stranger

Everyone tried to please people
they had never met before.

Realisation

Once you accept
that you are
> not forever,
then you can
> continue.

Explore the Unknown

Kiss me in *places*
you have never been.

Dancing Within the Fire

Love was luminous
and beautiful
but filled with mystery.

It left us stunned
as if a cosmic explosion of stardust
was blowing into our face.

Love took you by the hands
and danced around the Universe
as it was forming
for the first time.

It was the beginning of us,
but we did not know
that it would be
the start of our misery.

Someone, Somewhere

Someone was watching
the clouds go by,
and someone else was watching
the time.

Someone was telling a lie,
and someone else was writing
a rhyme.

Others were trying to get by,
and they were trying to appreciate life,
while many asked *why.*

Back at home, there was someone near
the kitchen sink, looking at a knife.
Alone and afraid. They were wondering why
nothing worked out for them,
as they started thinking about
ending their own life.

Sometimes you cannot stop
the tears from flowing.

Someone close to you was near
your bedside table.
They were always there.
With your eyes shut tight,
you smiled.

Someone else was laughing,
and someone across the park
      was dying;
nobody knew what was happening.

Someone was holding a cigarette,
thinking about smoking,
and someone else
was giving in to drugs.

    Should we have cared?

There was a patient who was watching
the birds sing near the hospital car park.
She was reminiscing about what life
could have been if she did not
      have cancer.

She did not survive.
She missed her daughter's birthday.

It was the choices we made
that we regretted in the end,
but we did not think
it could happen to us.

Someone loved you,
and someone cared.
Someone wanted to be there.

Someone was listening to the wind
in the park playground.
She was holding a flower,
watching the petals fall
as they thought about someone special.
She picked the petals
off a white daisy,
    "He loved me,
      he loved me not,"
    she sang.
She sighed as she pulled
the last petal from the daisy.

Did he know that she
was in love with him?
She wondered and looked
beyond the horizon.
He sat in his bedroom, thinking
about *someone else*
      that was not her.

The Universe looked after you,
and the cosmic dust that floated around
whispered a secret to you:
      "You will find someone
      who loves you one day,
      do not get distracted
      along the way."

Toxic

When we fell in love,
we started losing ourselves.

Missed Heartbeats

You felt your pulse
because you were not well;
your heart tugged
your skin back,
which pulled you to the side.

Something did not feel right,
    and your heart
        did not speak,
so it held its breath
to miss a beat
so that you could notice.

You peeked
and saw them hiding
behind the tree,
with their hair waving
from behind the trunk.
Your heart sped up,
dragging you from side to side,
missing every second beat.

You felt ill,
and your breathing
became more frequent
but irregular.

There was so much energy
inside your body;
you cannot see
from the outside.

You were in love.
This astounding phenomenon,
where one could transcend
space and time,
that was so immense,
your body acted
before it thought.

Powerful emotions that brought
your world into focus.
Your heart could move the harshest
and coldest mountains with what you felt.

Yet, the heart had the power
to drop the mountains
on top of you.

Holding hands with love
could be like watching the stars;
they might be there, shimmering,
      ready to live inside your heart
         or shoot off to orbit another galaxy.

Unsighted Hope

The *why*
is not important
because now,
you have the future
to wonder.

For Them

Do it for the ones
       you love
because you give them
       hope
when there is nothing
       left.

Writing Pain

I write
       so I can heal.
I hope you read this
so when you break,
like me,
       maybe,
we can be familiar
       together
and *believe*
       we will make it.

Translate

All she needed was someone that understood her.

Belated

There was no need for you to be afraid
of love.

      Say it
            before it is *too* late.

Breaking the Wall

You searched.

You had been waiting
      for someone.

Waiting for someone
that you would accept
      to let in.

The Burning Question

If I was God,
would I allow suffering?

The First Light of Day

There was a lurking fear
inside of us
when we had expectations.
Our unwillingness to move forward
if the haphazard hand of probability
went against our favour.

You started the day
when you opened your eyes,
hoping you could meet your
standards.

      Then the anxiety set in.
      You came to a halt.

It was beautiful outside,
but the hidden demons threatened another day.
Fear understood anxiety lacked compassion.
The demons had their own goals
and disregarded your
thoughts and
      feelings.

The demons tried to achieve their
to-do list.
     Just like you.

When walls surrounded us,
our souls felt trapped.

There was no sunshine,
but light seeped through
the gaps of the ragged edges
of the brick wall
that pierced our eyes.
We did not trust life,
     or anything.

What wandered inside our minds
when we were alone
was frightening.

When the ships had set sail
and abandoned you
with your suitcase on the pier,
     what did you do?

Where would you have gone
when your emotions became
too much?
How did you feel when humanity
did not seem to care?

What did you do?

Humanity cared,
    but it was not good
        at letting you know.

When humanity spoke,
words dribbled out,
and the words were empty shells;
for you to crawl inside.
They were inadequate
    because they came from humans.

You believed you were
a good person,
but a good person
did not get special treatment.

Being a good person was a choice
and what you believed was right.
Right and wrong was a
human-made concept.
Life and the Universe
did not revolve around
human-made concepts.
It did as it pleased
because it was indifferent
to everything,
whether something may be innocent
or seething with evil.
Your moral compass
set the path you picked.

Is that all we are?
A collection of atoms and molecules?
Who shed tears and struggle,
to fight for a life of endless pain
and to watch our
hopes and dreams
disappear.

For what purpose did we
continue to endure the
grind?

What if
we were an accident,
and we were here because we were
an outcome of an
infinite level of possibilities,
    but maybe
        not a very good one in that?
If we were an *accident,*
    are we meant to be helpless?
    Are we meant to be suffering
    and destined to die out?

We had no one else;
it was just us.
We were in our skins
every hour we were alive.
No one mattered
other than themselves.

Your experience and pain were unique
to your existence, and that was
one lonely experience.

When you broke parts of yourself,
they left you to pick up those pieces.
        Putting yourself back together,
no matter how sharp
and odd-shaped the pieces were.
        Life did not give discounts or benefit schemes.
        Life expected a standard with no emotion.
        The Universe was stern
        and did not show sympathy
        when galaxies devoured other galaxies,
        or when black holes swallowed light.
                There were no concessions.

Was this world worth fighting for?
Was life worth it?
Was the pain worth
the wisdom it gave,
compared to never being born
and experiencing these events?

To what extent did we bleed,
    to live,
        to breathe?
To go through ourselves
to find happiness
for a short while
before the balance of sadness
decided how happy you are.

Humans killed and conquered each other
so humans could set rules and order.
We funded the military to protect
    humans from humans.
That was what humans did.

We suffered
    because to suffer
        is to be human.
We felt pain
    because to feel pain
        is to be human.
To have existed,
    to have died
        is to be human.

That was the way.

Perhaps, it was better to start
the day doing nothing,
with an empty mind,
and let the Universe dictate
what our happiness and sadness
would be.

Around the Sun

"What do you think attracted your mother to your father?"

"The same stars
that brought us
together."

Promise

I was dying,
        waiting for the emptiness
            to take me.

Promise me you would
do better.

Do not waste your life.
        Do not take things for granted.

Fear Man

You yelled at her,
confused her.
She wanted love and kindness.
What you gave
was a reminder of men
to avoid when she grew older.

Creation

There was no date.
No time.

We appeared.

Time was not significant,
and we lived our lives without
illusion or constraint.
No commitments
or rules to obey.
We wanted to live
how we imagined.

A New Hope

Where did you go?
Where would you be?
Will you sail back home,
or venture out to sea?

Another place to find
a new you?

Where would you go,
when the place you called home
does not feel like home?

So many roads that led to uncertainty,
so many foreign places,
so many decisions made you unhappy,
and so many worlds that made you feel alone.

Where would you go,
when the burden did not ease
but became denser, the more you
wandered through the darkness?

The light did not follow you through
the end of the tunnel,
but you were waiting for it,
and it never arrived.

You watched every move,
        you made
every choice and every breath.
The light did not hold your hand
        or give you a map.
It shined through
when the abyss caught you,
and it became harder to move
and difficult to breathe.

That was when you needed light most.
Where hope was weak,
and the end felt close.

Something gave,
        and you took.

Home became clearer,
and the world healed.

No Shoes

Walk with me
up a thousand steps,
with your shoes off.
Loving me will *feel*
like that.

Gravity

I cannot stop looking
into your eyes;
the gravity
of
them
pulled
me
in.

Fading Time

The day started with
great anticipation.
As twilight bled into the night,
we had achieved little.
We struggled beyond our
wildest imaginations.
Our hopes and dreams laid bare,
disheartened on the edge of oblivion.

Crazy Love

I want to drink what is inside the Sun
and fill it back up with oceans.
I want to dig inside the Moon
and fill it up with fire.
I want the days to swallow me whole
and the nights to burn.

Without you
        anything I do
               is pointless.

Hard Knocks

You arrived with the storm;
battered from the wind,
but that did not stop you.
You continued to run
through the black woods
and to my doorstep.
        The horror you overcame
            just to see me.

Brine

You were the sea, and I could not swim,
so you slowed down the waves
        to let me in.

I thought you were gentle
        but cold at first.

As I went underneath you,
        I tasted salt.

The further I searched,
the more I discovered,
a vast and a
        rough sea.

If you were *expecting honey,*
        I was not it.

People liked to lose their thoughts
when they looked at me,
but once they went in,
they disliked
        the taste of me.

No More Words

You say too much
when you should just
kiss me.

Feeling Alive

In moments where
I cannot speak,
I wrote words for you
because you were unique.

I did not know you well;
but if we did,
the chemistry between us
would tell.

Some people dug themselves
      further into a hole
when involving love.
They did not know
what falling in love felt like
because they were on the ground,
      digging
           instead of leaping.

We did not waste the day
getting stuck in ridiculous things.

You thought of me and my words.
You thought of me as if you have
      never met me before.

You saw me as if you have never
      wanted to see anyone else anymore.

Puddles

I peeled layer by layer of myself
to get rid of all the places you touched.

I tried to love,
        and I failed.

I needed to unlearn
who you were and pretended you never existed.
I have forgotten our love,
and once all traces of you have vanished,
I will have a new shell.
A shell that is tougher than before,
a wall taller and more durable,
so when the next person comes along,
it will be harder for them
to see my holes.

Shaping Clouds

I watched the clouds to pass the time.
I saw you in every formation.
     Your eyes and
             your lips
were coming together
like you were watching me from afar
but close to home.

I whispered the words I love you,
and the letters floated away
from my mouth and into the sky.
They drifted with elegance
     and landed inside a cloud
          that was in the shape of your heart.

Without a Touch

Your eyes want to
undress me.

Silence Sounds Better with You

I obsessed over you.
You thought I was not listening,
but I was getting lost in everything
    that was
        you.
    Your eyes,
    your smile,
    the way you played with your hair
    and how you looked at me.

I traced the lines on your lips,
and you dismantled my thoughts.
I was once good at conversation
    until I met you,
and ever since,
    I have been silent.

Born

There was no greater reason
to celebrate
than your birth.
There was no greater miracle
than breathing.
Knowing you existed
brought colour back
into my world.

You found me and
      gave me warmth.

As we aged, I feared
that one day all this
would end,
all our achievements,
the mounting adversities
and all the carefree moments.
All this, we would not have had
the experience and continued happiness
      unless you were born.

It all started because
you were born.

Live to Love

If you only live once,
why give in to lust?
Love needs the madness
to work in a short life,
do not waste
        love.

There is an empty seat here
for you to watch
the raindrops
and how they hit the ground,
        to an ant,
        it is a tidal wave of dreams
                never realised.

The little
        things
                count.

Speechless

I could not speak
when you looked at me.

Lovers Part Way

One of the most fearful aspects
of being in a relationship
is its unpredictable change.
One day you could wake up, and the love disappears.
Everything you have could be for nothing.
As if this adverse change occurs
because that one person is not your soul mate.
You remove this person from your life,
and they become
      new again.

Finding Meaning

You can walk along,
feeling nothing,
if feeling
      is something
you want to do.

You should find
what makes you
whole.

What Does Progression Look Like

We were born crying,
     hello, world.

Preschool,
     I cannot remember it.

Primary school,
weeping to a certain point
until first grade
and then alone
because no one liked me.

High school,
     annoyed and disappointed.

University,
high hopes led
to broken dreams,
still annoyed and
even more disappointed.

Career.
Partner,
maybe children.
Promotion.
Mortgage.
Broke.
Heartbreak.
Reminisce.
Retire.
Death,
  tears,
    and alone.

"Am I progressing towards death?"

"Why are you looking at the end?
If you look at the end,
then you are already dead."

The progression looks like this.
To progress,
  I need to live,
  but I was afraid
  it would end.

I am afraid of being afraid.

It is simple.
The only obstacle is me.

Effortless

You picked at the scabs
to *hide* what was
underneath.
You did not need to
hurt yourself over beauty.
It was always there.

Fire and Rain

The music played,
      and you left.

I was awake during
the darkest part of the night.
      There was no wind,
but a calm passing of melody,
      until the music faded.
You could only hear
the crashing of waves
against a bed of rocks.

      She was the fire
      that soon went out
      with the soft rain
        that passed by.

Life in Monochrome

Life
        needed
                colour.
Bright enough
to have made you
        wonder.

We enjoyed fantasising
about the ideal life—a
        luxurious big house
        with crystal chandeliers.

Sometimes the tall ceilings
were hard to reach,
and they remained dark.

Build the
l
        a
                d
                        d
                                e
                                        r

that could reach the sky,
for when you need it,
your ladder will be ready.

What You Sea

The light of another day
grew dim,
as I spent it on
overthinking.
All the ideas I had
became nothing
as I dismantled their existence.

In a state of wonder,
        I thought,
what if the Universe had forgotten
when it created us?
        Did it think,
                or perhaps
                        it took a view of indifference
                        when it made us.
Did it know what it was doing,
        or did it
        wave its cosmic wand
                and *hocus-pocus*,
        out came dark energy
                and dark matter.

The Universe
>> painted to
>>> let off steam,
but the picture was missing the details.
The Universe, just like an artist,
>> splashed
>>> confusion
>>>> and disorder
>>> on a canvas,
>>> awaiting until the clouds formed
>>> to see the masterpiece.

Go through life without holding
>> ransom to ideas,
>> let the thinking run
>> its beautiful imagination
>> within yourself.
>>> Grab hold to every thought
>>> and make it rain chaos.

The sea appeared empty from the top,
but there was so much happening

below.

Genesis

CHAPTER 2

SUNSET

The end can arrive as soon as the beginning.

There is no guarantee
of survival.

How long is unknown.

How you occupy your time
is at your discretion.

Fate controls the power
to influence the end.

You will not change the end.

You cannot stop the end.

Sunset

The Way We Hurt

I like hurting you,
and I do not know why.

I am your poison,
and you will not leave.

I will continue to torment you
because in my sick mind
     I enjoy it,
and *you* will not understand why,
and *I* will not understand why.
We will both
     go
          on
confused and destructive
until one of us cannot take it anymore
and breaks the cycle,
     ends the chaos,
          faces up to the fear
               and leaves.

Silence

I spoke too loudly, and now;
I do not speak
at all.

Living in Pain

Hurt,
so your heart felt
what was
             missing,
what it
      lost.

We needed to feel as if
we were reaching
        towards the skyline,
so we knew
        what it felt like
                to be alive.

Time

The clock was ticking.
The years had gone by.

My heart cried,
        and hers lied.

Wandering Eyes

I wanted to swim and dance
around your lips.
You did not smile
but waited for me to stop.

Your eyes hid secrets from me
as if you knew the location of Atlantis
and did not want to show me.
You clouded your thoughts
and brought me such pain
that if my heart were bone,
it would have splintered.
I would have drowned searching
for the beautiful things that lurked
inside your magnificent mind.
Instead, you threw me a life jacket
to keep me from diving in
      your Mariana Trench.

You wanted to talk,
but with someone else.

Our conversations were
    short and   distant.

Once we were inseparable,
    but now,
        our end was
           inevitable.

Escape

I understood why you left.
I had personal development issues;
I felt humiliated and pressed
my head against my pillow,
wanting to escape this world.

I was off to a disappointing start,
but you were too far ahead of me,
and I could not catch up.

It was hard for you;
contemplating living the rest of your life
with me was not the smartest idea.

You hid your thoughts,
went through the breakup alone
and kept our demise a secret.
        I failed to pick up on the signs.
My stubbornness
could not see how destructive
our relationship was.

You explained we needed to part
for our sanity,
to leave the relationship behind
and find someone new.

You were a fish in a pond,
but when I dipped my toes,
you swam away.

I wanted you, but I cannot
figure it out.

Are You There

You search for your
first love
in everyone.

Wilted Memories

I had forgotten what you looked like.
Once upon a time, you took my heart,
    danced with it and
tore it apart inside.

All things end,
    but it still hurt.

I had memories of you,
    but they faded,
    and the days were short and empty
    without you in them.

Time was escaping *so fast*
that it felt like I cannot contain the leak.
    I was watching you fall away;
    I was watching the colours fade.
    I forgot what it was like
        to touch your skin;
    I forgot what your
    smile looked like.

These memories of you
seem to have disappeared,
and I cannot control this state of decay.

When I looked into your contemplative eyes,
     I saw your sadness.
     You could not speak;
        or blink.

You looked at me, upset and said,
     "It is okay. I am okay with what is
     happening to me. It is okay."

I am afraid that I would forget
the way you acted,
your mannerisms, the sound of
your voice and the look in your eyes
when you smiled at me.

I missed the way you had
made me a better human.
I regretted that I could not
have helped you become
a better version of you.
You were too busy
     working on me,
        and I was selfish.

I tried to keep your thoughts near;
your picture was never far away
because when my memories of you disappeared,
I wanted mementoes of you
to keep you near.

What I had always feared
had come true,
but it was that negative energy that pushed
         the hands of luck away from us.
The self-fulfilling prophecy
was complete.

Time continued to take your memory away,
stealing whatever trace, I had of you,
and the leftover particles
of your scent.

I would have given everything away
to have heard your voice again.
To see what your smile
would have looked like
and what we could have been.

Playing in the Den

We hoped to move on,
get the day started and enjoy life.
No matter how tall we built our walls,
we put on the smiles,
but we were drowning inside,
battling to breathe every minute of the day.

There lived a significant ache and hurt that appeared
in the morning and at night.
We lost a connection,
and we became disconnected.

The broken people
remained lost because
what broke was a part of them.
      You never get that back.
You say goodbye to everything you were before
and say hello to the *you*, after.

We lived to cope with misery;
      it was temporary,
but temporary soon became permanent.

How quick a beautiful life
became sour.

How cruel could the Universe be?

There was no mercy.
Indifference inhabited all,
but indifference was not something
I comprehended.
I thought there was something else out there
trying to get me, and when I asked why,
    it gave me silence.
In silence, nothing existed,
and in nothing,
arrived pain.

The Bitter End

Every moment I held you,
the *look* on your face
hurt me.

Poison

How could you be
    so toxic
when I was
    in love with you?

I Wish It Was Love

He fingered her heart,
cutting
    her
        insides,
with not a care
for her well-being,
or how
she was feeling.

Art

We were both pieces of artwork
hanging
off a canvas.
We could not understand
each other.

Handmade

I made you things,
and you did not care.

Go

If I cannot make you stay,
then go.

If my love could not keep you,
then nothing, I could do
will make you.

A Fairy-Tale End

He waits for you at your front door,
thinking of lines to tell you
about how he feels.

Even when raining outside,
he will not leave in the cold
without telling you.

She looks outside,
watching him from the start,
slowly as the raindrops;
the drop that falls
    from
        his
           heart.

She thinks that leaving him behind
    would be better.
She conceives it would be better
    if he would die alone,
and he believes it would last forever.

The rain kept on falling,
and she admires the perfect day.
She smiles anyway,
even when he is not there.

He is so cold sitting by her front door,
finding it hard to breathe and wondering
why the door never opens.
Wondering if she is the air
that he lives on and yet,
he is spending his entire life wondering.

She looks outside,
watching him from the start,
slowly as the raindrops;
it drops right
      from
           his
                heart.

She is spending her whole life dreaming.
He is spending his life waiting by her front door.
Both are never finding their worlds of make believe.

The rain never stopped for years.

He wonders how she is,
asking how her life worked out.

He is still waiting for her to come out
as he sits by her front door.

He is quiet and wondering if everything will be okay.

She looks outside for the last time.
Watching him until the end,
slowly,
as the raindrops;
it was the *last* drop that
fell
from
his
heart.

Killing You

The sound of my name
made it hard for you to
b r e a t h e.

Living Inside Your Head

Nothing made sense to me anymore,
but you made sense.

I stared at the mirror
and who I saw
was disappointing.
You suffered from the same
self-esteem issues too.
When you looked into the mirror,
you cannot see how beautiful you were.

You were not the same person
I fell in love with all those years ago,
and I feared we had grown   apart.

I lost touch with reality,
going in and out of
            consciousness.

Whether you were real or not,
I was unsure.
Perhaps my mind was becoming volatile,
unable to keep the peace that we had.

Nothing else mattered but you.
I had you believe
that there was no one else capable
    of loving you
        than me.
You doubted that based on probability.

Whatever your reasons were to leave me;
    they were valid,
    but I am not
    who you thought I was.

You created everything about me
inside your imagination.
Your mind was not happy anymore
with how I had interacted
with your thoughts.
Your head was telling you
to leave me.

Nothing was real unless you gave it meaning.
When you give something meaning,
you can take it away.

That is how something
becomes nothing.

A Broken Angel

There was a little girl
who walked at night,
with bourbon, her best friend
when she needed a break from life.

The boys called her an angel
with a smile,
but she could not fly
with broken wings.

A smile turned upside down
as she sang.
She walked alone through city lights.
　　　She cried
　　　as the bottle fell
　　　from
　　　　　　her
　　　　　　　　hand.

The world was in slow motion
when she fell asleep.
She had nightmares

and panic attacks when she slept;
she had no place to rest.

She had pain in both worlds;
her life was a mess.

She prayed to God,
pleading to make everything alright,
even though she was an atheist.
God did not respond,
and hope f a d   e   d.

She laid on the grass and
looked at the stars.
She wondered if her destiny
would have been different
in another universe.

The Sun slept in,
and she woke up confused.
A single
            drop
                    of
                            bourbon

was all that she could muster
in the bottle.

Even *bourbon* had abandoned her.

Her innocence stolen;
taken away against her will.
Her heart and mind
all fell apart.

She wandered down to the ocean;
to see her reflection.
The water was darkest at night.
Tears filled her eyes
        and stumbled down
from her cheeks,
filling her empty bottle of bourbon.

Her eyes reflected broken windows
that housed a child that used to
        laugh and smile.
The tears told a sad story
with no home to call her own.
The red stains on her white dress

filled her mind with madness.
She burned out;
all the flames vanished
        from inside of her.

The night sky bled darker.

        You cut the stars;
        they spilled black
        which moved like tar.

It became darker
        and darker.

Her hands sunk into the sand;
she caressed the grains in her palms.
She laid on the beach
and looked at the night sky again,
                in darkness,
hummed a song her mother
used to sing to her.

        As she slept,
        in her dreams,

everything was a mess;
she sleeps in Heaven now,
a place where she can rest.

Staying for Nothing

I lied to comfort you,
but we were never
going to make it.

Kiss the Sky

I saw what stress did to you,
my friend,
    how it wilted
        you away.

I saw your smile deteriorate.
I watched the flickering light behind
your eyes fade to black.
I felt pain when I heard
background murmurs of your name,
but I could not get you out of my mind.

Nothing distracted me when there was
a black hole in front of me
feeding on my soul.
It dressed in darkness
decorated with digested galaxies,
which filled me with fear and sadness.

I took long walks to clear my mind,
but that made it worse.

The ocean waited for the clouds
to kiss that day.

I had forgotten what it was like
to feel normal again.
I wanted to escape from this hell.

The time we had was valuable.
When we took our last breath,
it was tragic
as we had no choice
 but to give in,
 and give up,
 all we had known.

Nothing lasted forever,
but I hoped it would.

Fear was there, walking along
the city streets with me.
Watching my shadow and my eyes
crawl to the back of my head,
hoping fear did not walk me home again.

I watched you go,
and I felt remorse,
I should have never
let you leave home.

You committed your time
to what you loved
and exposed your feelings
for the world to see.

You hated control, and they
       tested you,
       tested your loyalty.

You both grew apart
from the struggle;
your stubborn ideals
separated you
and expectations
were not realistic.
She felt like you did not care
to see her grow.
       You did not even notice
       how she committed herself

to you, in every way
she could.

She looked for a key
that did not exist
to release her.
She was there wondering
when the torment would stop.
Her internal screaming
had nowhere to go.
Seething inside,
she felt dirty for trusting you.

She stayed too long
and lost respect in her relationship.

How long was *too* long?
If you were asking this question,
it was already too long.

My Struggle

You never believed
in me,
      to be
           with me.

I devoted everything,
put all my words
and what I felt for you
out there.

You ignored, and
you controlled me;
it was not fair,
but you tried to,
and that hurt me.

We grew   apart,
and we did not even try to find
the spark that we once had.

We became trapped;
     we both failed
to set each other free.

We lived like our problems
would not go away
with every argument.
We screamed at each other
        and cried alone
about the dream we never had.

We became stuck because
we could not say no,
even though
we were not compatible;
we had so much to learn.

In a disconnected
        and unobservable universe,
you would be with someone,
like me, but complete,
with their life together.
They would treat you right,
the way you deserved,
something I could not have
        given you.

Late

I was waiting
for you,
but you never came.

Break

I remember how
it used to be.
About what we had.
What we worked for,
we had genuine progress.

We went all in,
and it fell a p a r t.

Contagion

Lying in bed,
        crying out.
The shadows try
to capture my soul.

My tears are fighting,
but paralysed,
        from fear.

Find Me

I was going to jump,
and no one could stop me,
but I liked to think someone would.

Thinking about jumping was easy,
but it was a
      long

            way

                 down.

I opened the window
and conversed with the wind.
The wind did not want me to jump;
there was an unrelenting force
that pushed me back.
      Why did it bother to save me?

No one knew
that I was suffering
and nobody had noticed.
      Nobody understood.

It was easy to think about dying
inside my head, but nobody was
looking within my four walls
to see if I was okay.

The Dead Walking

They had not made it.

The bones all looked the same.
What was their story,
who did they leave behind?
Where did they go,
did they walk this path alone?

Life distracted them,
even though they were
heading towards the end.
     They arrived
without even knowing it
as if life injected them
with an anaesthetic agent
that made them numb.

Discarded

You stood there as you said your goodbyes, and you just threw me away.

Staying to Leave

With all that happened,
you stood by me,
hoping you and me
will somehow make it.

It was hard to live life,
knowing that we were at the cusp
of deteriorating.
Hard to love when we had
made up our minds to leave.

Salty Waters

I did not mean to make it hard for you.
I did not want you to feel this way,
but you told me to move on with my life
as your tears slipped
down
         your cheeks.

The Plan of Breaking

You were my lesson
I had to learn.

I found out you
had to leave.
It was part of the Universe's
hellish plan to show how
inadequate I was for you.

I had to destroy us to learn,
and it had to be you,
so I remembered what I lost.

No More

Losing you was the saddest part.

The *you*
    I knew
        does not exist anymore.

Panic

I walked through winter,
and I could feel her cold hands
        suffocating me
as if I was dragging along large,
sharp stones.

I was sinking in the cold,
along with my warm heart
that melted the snow
surrounding me.
With so much snow withered away,
it left an ocean that overwhelmed me
and closed in on my anxiety.

I felt depression's heavy hands
strangling me.
        I breathed too fast;
        I breathed too slow,
either way,
I tried to hold on to hope;
trying to come up for air.

Although I have fought through the wind,
I have seen how far I have grown.
There was nobody left to lean on.
    I panicked,
        and it scared me,
how the fragility of becoming broken.
required no effort.

I cannot break away from
worry and disappointment
when I sank on my own,
in the deepest end,
        alone.

Pretend

I knew you would disappear one day.
You extinguished the fire
and moved on.

I had placed you to the side of my mind
and pretended to forget
that you were the reason
I woke up smiling in the morning.

When I tried to sleep,
I closed my eyes
and lied to myself.
I attempted to tell my aching body
that I did not yearn for the warmest part
of your touch
missing on the empty side
of my bed.
I acted like you were not
the happiest part of me,
the one who made me realise
that I could feel alive.

I pretended that you were
easy to find, but somehow
you seeped through the tiny pores
in my chest and
                        spilled into my heart.

I sat here at night and pretended
you were not the person I wanted
to spend the rest of my life with.

Drought

There were no more tears
left in my eyes.
They had run out
for you.

If Eyes Could Speak

Her eyes were telling me something
that I cannot understand.
The sadness in her silence
    b r o k e
        my heart.

Birthday Remains

She never thought he
got her a birthday present.

    In the car crash,
they found torn pieces of wrapping paper
and the leftovers of a birthday card that read:
    I love you.

Junkyard Hearts

Where did all the broken hearts go?
A junkyard to console
each other?
A place where they exchanged their stories
while beating together to the same irregular beat
when they were in love.

They have missed moments,
moments they could have had together,
but now those hearts are somewhere far away.

Each day the distance
grew   further,
and the feelings became weaker.
The longing and tight spaces
between their arteries
were closing in.

These hearts tried to move on,
        but they did not.
They were stubborn,
        just like *you*.
The hearts haemorrhaged,

not for someone new,
    but for *you*,
until they were empty.
They experienced sorrow,
and they were delicate.

A stubborn heart was deadlier
    than a sledgehammer
striking a thin sheet of glass.

Falling
out of love with you
was the
thin
    sheet
        of glass
bracing for impact.

A Reminder to Give Notice

I hid within myself,
went inside my body and found
all the nooks and crannies
to lock my emotions in.

When you departed,
I knew where I would be.

I have furnished those places,
so the end did not hit so hard.

Could you tell I had not been
present in our relationship?

I was thinking about you leaving
than building on what we had.

With you, I felt like
I could move solar systems,
         and I feared
I could not anymore.

We were not perpetual,
    but temporary,
and the pain of that
was too much for me to take.

Peeling a Black Hole

When you stopped loving me,
      I peeled away.
I bent and twisted
      until I came off.
All that stuck was the
sticky residue I left behind.

You did not notice me when I was there.
Now that I am gone,
you might feel the draft from the window
where I used to sit.
You might hear a pin drop
from the emptiness of your heart.

You will not remember our time together
or the happiness we had.
Everything was a distant memory,
that was once alive.

      All that remained was
      the dark
          and cold,

from the bitterness
and hate
we created.

Indecisive

You cannot have me
and then
have me.
You are there
or you are not.

The Spider's Web

I lived in these days
disturbed and anxious
about your absence.
There was no sign of you.

You pulled a Houdini
and vanished.

You fell through
where I could not fit.

Letting go was your magic trick.
How did it feel away from me?
Did your parachute lessen your fall,
or was it like us,
falling too fast,
without control
or consequence?

You thought we were a mistake,
so you panicked and left,
disappeared in a puff of smoke.

I wanted to save us,
but these sticky webs blocked my way,
I got stuck, and I had to turn back.
I cannot go
where you spun these traps,
    in wickedness,
        without me.

I was running towards you
because my heart
did not find another way.
I kept getting caught in your webs
while you forgot about me.

The Morning After

The morning arose,
and you disappeared
with the night.
> Our love,
>> a chapter ended.

Everything I wrote
had no meaning since you left.

Whenever I spoke,
> I sighed,
and all the nights I spent alone
with the Moon
and woke up to the Sun
without your warmth.
> I was cold,
even when the rays of the Sun
> were piercing my skin.
I used to roll over
and find comfort knowing
you were there.
> Everything felt right,
> and now,

the summer air feels like
the dread of winter.

Three Hours

It has been a long time
since I last tasted food
or felt the drops of water
on my tongue.

My vision was hazy from debris,
but seeing was
            unnecessary to understand
what was happening.
The noises became familiar;
they became my eyes.

It was the norm to hear
            gunfire,
homing missiles and
            loud explosions
            where I live.
            It was everyday life.
The screams were deafening at first,
            but then
                        they became silent.

Many people died in wars.
They left behind those who loved them.
    Parents,
        wives,
            husbands,
                children,
            brothers,
        sisters and
    friends.

If you survived the war,
you became traumatised and numb.
The soldiers left their minds
on the front line,
and what they saw
could not be unseen.

Three hours was all we got
for a cease-fire in a place like this.

The food relief agency
dropped life-saving supply crates,
but they remained unopened.

Some containers did not make it
to their destination.

No one realised
  that there was no one left
     to open them.

Stay with Me

You can wait for someone
that is willing to stay,
or you can find someone
who *will* stay.

Wayward Thoughts

I heard your voice;
I saw your eyes.
You touched my hands;
you sang to my lips.
We became silent
when the light went out.

We smiled.

You looked towards the day,
watched as the Sun rose
and pondered whether
we seemed different.

Different Frequencies

It was hard for me
to hold back emotion.
I felt it all
      without diluting the feelings.

I put in everything I had,
and then you watched me burn
because you did not feel the way I did.

When you left,
      I broke.

The Dark Wizard

All that remained of me was this.

My skin had withered away.
My hair lost its memory.
I could see my wrinkles
from a distance,
and the dust was living
in the crevices.
My body lost the war against disease.
My eyes fell at the hands of cataracts
and its vast army of glaucoma.
My bones held their own,
but arthritis could go all day.
Plaque barricaded my arteries,
and the Trojan horse called junk food
blindsided me.

I visited the hospital
as if it were my second home.

Throughout the wars,
there were battles inside
my mind.

I was anxious and experienced
panic attacks.

Alzheimer's was lurking,
I knew the dark wizard could erase words,
thoughts,
      feelings,
           dreams, and
      everything
and everyone
      you ever knew,
             ever loved.
Alzheimer's was a constant fear,
worrying that one day you could fall
into a state of paralysis.

My lungs had no escape.
The enemy was invisible;
they released a slow poison
that climbed in the air.
We had no choice but to
breathe
      the smoke.

It was silent
    but took the vulnerable.

I thought about death a great deal.
I looked beyond,
with no focal point,
just breathing
and enjoying the moment.

To keep us alive, we had to take
prescribed medication.
We knew the medicine
was killing us, but the cost
to stay pain-free was worth it.
It was better to live one day
without the hurt
than to persevere in agony.

My weapon of choice was a walking stick.
It helped me to move,
to appreciate every detail and moment
that I was too busy to notice.

I discovered parts of life
that had passed me by,
like moments in a song.
After a thousand listens,
you hear a piece you had never heard before.

We had time to ponder.

The little things preoccupied me,
and I ignored the things that mattered.

After reminiscing about my life,
regrets did not appear to be
a big deal anymore.
Any wrongs, morals or values I had,
did not seem so important.

I questioned religion
and made amends with God
        to believe again,
        to live on after I die.
I needed comfort, even after
I denied it all these years.

I craved to be young again,
to see new technology,
and the unknown discovered.
    I accepted I would not get this chance.

I sat on the empty park bench
and reached out to my last thought.
I wondered about the good things
that I had done and achieved in my life.

I lived a good life.
I was happy.
I was ready to leave,
but others were not so lucky.

A Repeating Loss

I fear that I am losing you,
losing you in the same
way that I had lost
everyone else.

Losing the War

When she passed,
I did not just lose her;
       I lost every moment.
I lost every memory
that we could have had together.
I lost the person who she could have been
and the person I would have become
because of her existing.

I lost who I was,
and I was grieving
for what *we were*
when we were happy.

Sunset

CHAPTER 3

SUNRISE

The cycle continues,
and the beginning ends.

The end begins.

In your life, you might
live for a prolonged period.

You will experience so many
new days that will make you smile.
It is those days you remember.
It is those moments
that make life worth living.

It is the memories you make
that you will recall.

Sunrise

The Greatest Feeling

She could not comprehend
     love,
and she did not know
where to discover it.
She could not perceive
the sensation
or how to keep it.
She thought love
had to
     transcend everything
she had ever felt before.

Another You

Do not pity yourself.
Do not wait for the world
to save you.
Change comes from within,
      inside of you,
not from a person
          but deep inside you.

You will find what you are lacking,
and you will wake up in the morning ready.

For everything that you need
has always been
      inside of you.

Fire and Water

I was a raging inferno,
but when you looked
into my eyes,
I melted into water.

Orchestrated Chaos

If the Universe overthought everything it did,
    would it suppress ideas like us?
Would the Universe have
    destroyed itself
        by breaking down its thoughts
           enough to e x p a n d
                at the speed of light?
Would it have taken over itself
by drifting galaxies apart,
ripping their atoms away from themselves
and collapse?

Every planet could have
    exploded
    because the Universe could not let go
    of its obsessive
    thoughts.

As elegant and powerful as the Universe is,
it did not wander around with an anarchic mind
orchestrated to tear itself
    from existence.

The Universe had grand ideas;
    it did not overthink,
but moved on,
    expanding its mind.
It let its magnificent creations
    live their life
and watched

                from a distance.

You have a beautiful mind
    entangled in chaos,
just like the Universe,
    and filled with stars.

Kiss the Night

You found peace when you felt her heartbeat
on your chest and when her fingers
ran
d
    o
        w
            n
                your spine.

She was right there,
      defenceless.
That was when you knew she had given
herself to you.

She had secrets that she will not share.
I knew I would open her hidden
treasure chests in time,
and she would throw away
the keys.
I would see her glowing beauty and read
her closed book.
She was afraid that I would find out
how delicate she was,

how much she feared
letting someone in.

I wanted them to know you.
I wanted to travel around your world
and lie on the grass.
When people thought of me,
they would think of you.

When I held you in my arms, I wanted to
expand my lungs to let you all in.
I would have made your heart skip again.
With me, you could see through
the darkness with the excitement
dawning over your eyes
that would have made you feel alive.

I had seen lightning.
It was not as bright as you;
it did not strike as hard
          as you did.

I had seen masterpieces,
but they had not discovered

all the colours painted
living inside of you.

I was time-poor; I could feel my life
slipping through you.
      I was anxious;
      I was nervous
because I never had quality
time with you.

I spent days counting down the time
until I saw your sweet face.

In the short time I had on Earth,
you found me skipping down
      the busy city streets.
I found a quiet place
across the road,
sitting on a park bench
      thinking about you.

I wanted to kiss the sky,
kiss the night and end up in your arms,
      kissing you.

They called me mad,
but I did not care what they thought
when I was dancing to my beat,
    on my two feet.

This love was unpredictable.
I could have spent my entire life
running across your neck and
longing for you
    for all eternity.

Safe

I did not appreciate
what being secure
felt like
until I met you.

Alien Love

We could get lost in the city somewhere,
hide a bottle of wine
and get drunk together.

Hang from a tree and
      search for stars.

I did not know where
you came from,
but I hope you could point
to the night sky
and tell me which direction
you fell from.

Sweet End

Love was not bitter
when I tasted your lips.

Love did not hurt
when we danced inside
the apocalypse.

Hope

"What does love look like?" He said.

"Hope, it looks like hope.
I have been staring at hope for all this time.
That is what you look like to me." She said.

Comfort in Sound

I have so much to say to you,
       but I say nothing at all
because hearing your voice
makes me feel safe.

Fine Art

I look at you
like I look at art.
I can stare for hours
when we are far

                                        apart.

Do Something Real

Follow your heart
and not the delusion
created by the world.

Moving On (Part One)

I did not remember
what you felt like,
and I am completely fine
with that.

Taking the Punches

Life is pain, and we all feel it.
We can learn from it
and become distant from reality.
This pain can b r e a k us
back into our
      atoms and
          molecules
where picking up the pieces
may seem impossible.

We can survive the impossible
and be less afraid;
we can even be ready
for what life does
next.

No Justice

I am proud of you
for smiling,
for braving the harshness
of the world;
when life stole
your baby away
from you.

Shiver

Play with my hair
and run your fingers
down

     my

         spine.
Sometimes I need
the simple touch.

Love Thyself

I have been
      alone
all this time.

I thank my solitude
that I became
in love with myself.

A Light Push

If the dark should interrupt what we do,
then let the light inside our hearts
      push us through.

Loving Minds

He needed to see
what was inside your mind
before he stepped forward
for a kiss.

Skyline

If you want to love,
love without compromise.

Do not fear the hurting
because when your heart's palpitating
    in the twilight,
you will not fatigue;
      you will not be in the dark.

Let the heart *fall* in love.

Love Letters

You could save me,
and we will never say goodbye.

You could be my hero,
and we could fly.

A Blue Moon

Observer: Have you seen the sky today, sir?

Busy Man: No, I do not have time to see the sky!

Observer: Have you ever looked at the sky?

Busy Man: Why, yes, I have.

Observer: Is it beautiful?

Busy Man: It is just a sky.

Observer: How often do you look at the sky, sir?

Busy Man: Not usually. I am very busy!

Observer: What colour is the sky?

Busy Man: Surely you could take a peek?

Observer: I cannot see it.

Busy Man: It is not hiding, you know, it is right above you!

Observer: It hides from me!

Busy Man: No, the sky does not hide from anyone. We are all under it!

Observer: How about the blind?

Busy Man: You are blind?

Observer: Yes.

Busy Man: Well then, do not most things hide from you?

Observer: Most things. Except for emotions, I feel those.

Busy Man: Let me describe the sky for you. It is mostly blue. Sometimes, when the clouds arrive, it is white.

When the clouds turn grey, it upsets the sky. Other times, the sky paints in several colours depending on its mood. Just before sunset and sunrise, it has shades ranging from yellow, purple, orange and red. When the Moon makes its way past the clouds during the evening, the sky becomes black. If it is a clear night, you can see stars that twinkle like diamonds. When the Moon is blue, the sky might show you a shooting star. Sometimes people make a wish when they are lucky enough to witness one.

Observer: It sure sounds beautiful.

Busy Man: Yes it does, I have never spoken about the sky like this before; you have my gratitude.

Observer: Your gratitude?

Busy Man: Yes. Just now, I have realised I have been on autopilot for most of my life, doing all the busy things people do. I have not taken the time to appreciate the sky or my family for that matter.

Observer: You still have time. You cannot change what has happened, so change what is to come!

Painting the Night Sky

She laid down and pondered about painting
her bedroom ceiling to look like the night sky.
    Instead, she wrote words,
        dragging the ladder around her room,
        disfiguring the wooden floor
        as she became exhausted.
She wrote about her life
and what her childhood was like
to have grown up watching the stars at night.

Once she finished, she threw herself
on her bed and smiled.

She was happy because every time she was sad,
she could run to her room.
She could lock the door and look upwards,
where she remembered the life she had
and how much joy it brought her.

Her dirty fingernails
had a story of tenderness.
She went through hell to arrive

with a paint bucket
      filled with constellations.
She held on to the treasured
memories in her life.
She held on, no matter how knotted
her skin became
or how many volcanoes
      she jumped across.

When it rained ash,
      she planted flowers.

The Right One

I forgot the love
in the past
when I met you.

Repulsion

When you came closer,
     I moved   further away.
I know it killed you that I did,
but it was for the best.

     The closer you got,
     the further   I moved away.

No matter how hard you tried,
you did not make it far.

You were persistent,
but I did not fold.

Stopping Time

You become scared to overthink
everything about your life
because you realise it is now
      very beautiful,
and you do not want to
destroy it anymore.

Secure

I am not from here, but you
had made me feel like I belonged.
      A longing
I had never felt before.

Fading into Light

When everyone had forgotten about you,
    time
    will remember you.

When everyone had stopped listening,
    pray,
    and someone will listen.

Housewarming

Home is comforting because it is like
a big
    warm
        hug
when you are inside of it.

Passion

You enjoyed the battle of saying my name when our tongues intertwined.

Left Wanting

He needed to speak to her
when she was not around,
and she thought you never
wanted to talk to her.

He wanted you to notice
how you made his world
spin around, and she tried to tell him
she was feeling ignored.

> She thought,
> when they closed their eyes,
> they never believed they would
> experience a love like this,
> even though
> it was not perfect.

When she closed her eyes,
she did not dream,
and when he slept;
he wanted her to keep
that side of the bed warm.

They craved and fantasised
about being together.
When they were away
the distance was
      unyielding,
and the thoughts
      superficial.

She remembered the love
they had for each other,
      without fail,
and when he escaped lockdown,
      they embraced,
           and never let go.

Finding Comfort

One day they would get to know
the person you were and saw what you hid
beneath the disguise.

They tried to seduce your mind,
and you liked it, and perhaps
they might have been the one
to make you happy.

You had to go through
the flood to breathe because they
broke you into a thousand pieces.

It was hard to put yourself
together again,
      but you did.

You showed your cracks;
you were often alone,
and that was your genuine test.
Your heart struggled
to fight another contender.

It was essential for you
not to throw your world away,
but you wrote a song about it.
Words made you feel better
because they were familiar.
They became your friend
when human contact
    hurt the most.

My Pillar

You carried me
when I could not stand.

Safe Keeping

I kept you safe,
in a place far away
from the noise and
hidden dangers of the world.

I left you in an alleyway
of lost memories;
     you called it my heart.

Live Now

The biggest change you can make
to your life is to stop waiting for
the weekend.
Start living your life
as if it was the weekend
every day.

Warm Moments

I found infinite conversations with you.
We talked from one sunrise to the next,
and we did not tire of each other.

Beating Up Depression

Writing your emotions in a notebook
can be comforting,
but it is not the best way
to deal with feelings
that get you depressed.
Face them when you are ready
because it is when you defeat them
that you can begin to heal and grow.

When they come again,
they will remember
and run away from you.

Hide and Seek

Find peace in places
that do not give
you stress.

Licking the Wounds

The best thing you can do
is to keep positive.

You must train your mind
to move forward.
Do not forget about the sadness
that got you here,
but learn to live with it
so you can enjoy living again.

You need to tell yourself
        everything will be okay,
                because it really will be,
        and you alone have that control,
                        no one else.

Slowing Down

Sometimes we need someone to talk to,
and no one is there.
Do not become overwhelmed,
if you do,
      stop and think,
           and concentrate on your breathing.
Tell yourself,
the birds will sing,
      the Sun will rise.
I am *necessary* to the world;
      life needs me.
I am unique, a miracle from the stars
and the moon that controls all the tsunamis
in the oceans.
My life matters, my value and my worth,
is immeasurable.

You Hurt to Become Better

Every love lost
is a lesson to improve.

The Dependant

I dream because
you exist.

A Friend Up There

The mind is constant;
it does not rest.
It will lurk in the past;
it will feel nostalgia and capture emotions
that made you feel stress
and heartbroken.

Your mind does not want you to forget
the hardship you had in your upbringing,
but it needs your help to think positive.

The mind is alone up there,
and it requires you to be its friend.
It needs you to try;
      it *really* needs you.

The Act of Healing

Forgive yourself when you are
angry at the world.

Be kind to your soul;
there was nothing
you could do.

Complacency

They are not in love;
they do not pretend to be.

They love and hate the same.
They are comfortable.

Unchained

When you left,
you gave me the freedom
to be me.

My Balloon

I liked that you
      left the balloons
out for me.
It was a reminder
      that we would
float away
      together
            someday.

Moving on with Pain

You are worthy of a happy life
no matter the pain
you have been through,
no matter the cost.

The world is moving,
and you will relearn
to love yourself
and set your life
in motion again.

A Friend from Within

My body and I had many things in common,
but communication was not one of them.
My body was trying to speak to me,
but I misread them as
normal sensations.
        The hairs that stood up
        on my arms and back,
the shivers that rode up
on my spine.
        The sunken heart that kept
        me awake,
and the rush of emotions.
        The changes that happened
        when I fell in love,
the excitement and
the ecstasy.

The body kept us from the heavy burdens
that tried to stop us.
The body tried its best to help,
but we read the signs as
        something different.

We misunderstood the body.
Maybe it did not need interpreting,
but to be second nature,
an instinct akin to trust.

When the world becomes
debilitating,
listen to your body,
it will know what to do.

A Positive Life

You sparkle
in everything you do
to help keep
the darkness at bay.

Why Not You

You dictate to the world
when you are ready.
Go quiet into your life and engage
every opportunity you can,
  because you *can,*
   and you will.
Repeat out loud,
why not *you.*

Resilience

Life has broken you
like reading scathing critic.
It punched you
  in the face,
but here you are,
resembling a water-filled
training mannequin.
You spring back up,
  smiling,
   rebounding from adversity
    and moving on.

Illuminate

I lost my hope and faith
in everything.
The ordinary particles invaded a life
built for greater things.
   Then you came.
The light in the darkest part
of the night, where I was drowning
in an abyss, lurking and hoping.

Diamond

Nothing compared to you,
but I see how blinded I was,
that you were not
the end of the world.

I knew I would
find someone
   better than you.

The Garden

Her body grew flowers
when she got rid of
the weeds.

The Hero

You were perfect.

You did not worry
about first impressions.

You smiled, waved your hands
and lived in disguise
to hide the evil fighting inside.
The evil nobody recognised
because you wanted to
shield them from fear.
You felt it was your burden to bear.

You never gave up
because the cost of failure
was a heavy burden to bear.

You could not replace
what you had sacrificed.

The pressure claimed years from your life,
trying to live up to expectations.

You cannot keep living this way,
     but you did,
     because you cannot
     see a way out.

A day will arrive where your
strength will not be adequate,
and you will consider
leaving and giving up.
They will discover you
want to go.
They will watch
everything you do.

You hid behind a mask,
but you convinced yourself everyone
knew about your identity and plan.

Someone pulled the plug on you,
and you cannot help but feel
the overwhelming association
you had to the source.

Who spilled the truth
about you?

You knew who it was.
You felt betrayed.

You spent years faking an identity
that you had questioned
who you were.

It took one failure to unravel it all.

One mistake and
one lapse in judgement
to start the doubting.

Everything good
that you had done,
undone.

You were responsible,
courageous;
the role model
people admired.

You made one wrong move,
and everyone questioned
your righteousness.

You spent the aftermath in isolation;
the planet appeared duller,
and the people frustrated you.

Staying afloat in the fallout
was an expectation
for you to be strong,
even when you could
           not stand up.

Everything was yours to lose.

The fight was in your head.

To overcome pain,
you had to
           fight yourself,
and that kept you going.

Your relationships suffered.
Jealousy was prominent.
They were temporary,
and when they lasted;
  it was for pretend.

  You did not need saving.

You stood there,
in solidarity,
with one path to walk.
The ground shook.
  Your mind trembled
towards a place that made you feel at peace,
to escape the anxieties life had thrown at you.

They filled your days with earthquakes,
but that did not stop you
  from walking the path of healing.

Life Story

I was a book filled with
empty pages.
You saw my potential
and filled my life
with words.

Finding Strength

You knew everything about me,
and with that knowledge;
you crushed my soul.

There was more to this story.
I only saw it through my eyes.

She was reckless,
but she needed to save herself.

We did not need to die
with our situation;
we could have changed them.
No matter how permanent it felt,
our predicament was not.

Your destination was always varying.
Every decision you made along your journey
was altering where you end up.
If you had a peek at your future
at different points of your life,
you would change everything.

You guided every decision you made
by how you felt
    as if you belonged.
    Belonging was a place
where everyone was
searching for within themselves.

You waited through
trying circumstances.

It was hard to leave,
but you did it.

Awakening

You were the sun
missing in my sky.

Becoming Poetry

When I first met you,
I wrote poetry to express
how much of the Universe
reminded me of you.
Now we are together;
my words do not flow
as they should.

You thought our love
was not comparable to before,
and I hate how you believed that.
I craved your company,
and I wanted to exist
together as if
we were orbiting each other
in the vacuum of space.

Your eyes captivated me,
and I did not say a word.

I read everything you did
because you had become
the poetry in my life.

I did not want to miss a second
because a second lost
     was *enough* of you;
       I would be
missing.

Wellness

Smile when all is
not well.

Drops

Like a raindrop,
I was impure.

At the centre of me
lied debris from when I
fell through the sky,
and my emotions hit every
building in sight.

It was impossible to feel
the happiness that I did before,
but when the rain came,
I was still beautiful.

The Boundary

There is no limit on
how much you can win,
but the limit you
put on yourself.

Following Your Passion

What should you focus on,
       the goal or the journey?
If you focus on the goal,
you will make a lot of mistakes.
There is nothing wrong with that.

You could thrash about causing a riot
and send the Richter scale in an uproar,
but the focus you have on the journey
will measure your success.
The size of your dedication
       is as bright as a star.
The urge to push ahead of the pack
will become insignificant
with this drive and intensity.

If you focus on what you are doing,
rather than what you want,
you will get to the goal
without even realising it.

Keep doing what you are doing.

Even at your absolute best,
people will still criticise you.

Do what makes you happy.

The Space Time Filled: Volume 1

Sunrise

TERMINUS

The journey's end is not here, but we are closing a volume of this series. Like concluding chapters in our life, something more is unfolding, to explore and to discover.

It will challenge you to overcome what stands in your way. When you do, it will demand more of you, because the more you go in, the harder it becomes. You are on this path to understand more of your existence.

There will be an "Eclipse" when you are standing on top of towering mountains at "Midnight". The "Revelations" of every battle you have ever faced will make you think and feel more and more until we reach our ultimate destination.

Sit and see what lies ahead. An entire world needs your attention, celebrate your achievements and stop if you are busy to breathe in the air for a minute.

You are welcome to review and share your experience in reading this book on Goodreads, Amazon and on any other platform you choose. Please share your pictures and thoughts on my Facebook page and tag me on Instagram and Twitter.

Thank you so much for your support and thank you for reading *The Space Time Filled: Volume 1*, I am sure we will meet again soon.

.

Terminus

The World Begins with You

To my son, Lake.
This book started before you
and now ends with you.
Everything that I have written,
everything that I have felt
does not come close
to what you mean to me.
You are the closest thing
    to heaven.

When I am gone,
    or if I am not there,
take this book,
    keep it close.
For my heart and soul went into
creating it, the *same* ingredients
I used to make you.

Terminus

My Spark in the Dark

To Murphie, my daughter.
You weighed only 460 grams
when you were born,
but the weight of your heart
was heavier than
      the
            entire
                  Universe.

I look for you in the stars,
in search of your light.
Until then,
I lay submerged
      in the dark
            without you.

The emptiness you have left
is vast.
I could not fill the cavity,
but I stay hopeful.

I will keep the space
that you left warm for you
when you need rest
from your cosmic adventures.

In times where I cannot get through life,
you were the smallest spark
that shined to break the barrier
keeping me paralysed.

I wait for the day
where I can join you.
You have one hell of a story
to tell me and
          lost time to find.

Until then, my love,
you remain
my spark
          in the dark.

The Space Time Filled: Volume 1

Terminus

ACKNOWLEDGEMENTS

Thank you to Jacquie, for believing in me when I doubted myself. For motivating me when I could not continue to finish this book and for being my sounding board daily. I love you, dearly.

Thank you to my son, Lake. He loves books, and he does not know Dad has released a book. He reminded me about the miracle of life and taught me innocence again and to this day, teaching me so much more. The love I have for Lake continues to overflow.

Thank you to my daughter, Murphie. Life was not kind to you, and I could not save you. You gave me so much that I could not translate into words. My thoughts are with you every day, and now you are in my book forever. You gave me something to believe in and one day I will see you again.

Acknowledgements

Thank you to my family for supporting me and showing excitement for the release of my book.

To my readers, I am not capable of using words to show how much your support means to me. It is what has kept the creative writing flame lit.

You are all the reason this book is something tangible. You took my passion seriously and helped me put this book into your hands so you could hold and read the words from this page.

You showed me love when I needed love. You showed me support when I needed help, and for those reasons, *I did it.*

The Space Time Filled: Volume 1

Acknowledgements

ABOUT THE AUTHOR

Michael Daaboul is a lover of words, and a writer based in Melbourne, Australia. He has a bachelor's degree in design and a master's in creative writing from RMIT University. He shares his writing with the rest of the world at www.michaeldaaboul.com where millions of people have read his work. *The Space Time Filled: Volume 1* is his first published poetry and prose collection.

About the Author

INDEX

A

A Blue Moon, 157
A Broken Angel, 86
A Fairy-Tale End, 79
A Friend from Within, 181
A Friend Up There, 177
A Heaven You Never Knew, 3
A Light Push, 154
A New Hope, 32
A Positive Life, 183
A Reminder to Give Notice, 114
A Repeating Loss, 134
Alien Love, 149
Another You, 140
Are You There, 70
Around the Sun, 29
Art, 78
Awakening, 195

B

Beating Up Depression, 172

Becoming Poetry, 196
Belated, 20
Birthday Remains, 111
Born, 45
Break, 99
Breaking the Wall, 20
Brine, 37

C

Comfort in Sound, 150
Complacency, 178
Contagion, 99
Crazy Love, 36
Creation, 31

D

Dancing Within the Fire, 8
Diamond, 185
Different Frequencies, 128
Discarded, 103
Do Something Real, 151
Drops, 199

Index

Drought, 110

E
Effortless, 53
Escape, 68
Explore the Unknown, 7

F
Fading into Light, 164
Fading Time, 35
Fear Man, 30
Feeling Alive, 39
Find Me, 100
Finding Comfort, 168
Finding Meaning, 49
Finding Strength, 193
Fine Art, 150
Fire and Rain, 54
Fire and Water, 141
Following Your Passion, 201
For Them, 18

G
Go, 78
Gravity, 35

H
Handmade, 78
Hard Knocks, 36
Hide and Seek, 173
Hope, 150

Housewarming, 164

I
I Wish It Was Love, 77
If Eyes Could Speak, 111
Illuminate, 185
Indecisive, 118

J
Jubilant, 3
Jump into the Abyss, 6
Junkyard Hearts, 112

K
Killing You, 82
Kiss the Night, 144
Kiss the Sky, 92

L
Late, 98
Left Wanting, 166
Licking the Wounds, 174
Life in Monochrome, 55
Life Story, 192
Live Now, 171
Live to Love, 47
Living in Pain, 65
Living Inside Your Head, 83
Losing the War, 135
Love Letters, 156
Love Thyself, 154

Lovers Part Way, 49
Loving Minds, 155

M
Missed Heartbeats, 14
Moving On (Part One), 152
Moving on with Pain, 180
My Balloon, 180
My Pillar, 170
My Spark in the Dark, 211
My Struggle, 96

N
No Justice, 153
No More, 105
No More Words, 38
No Shoes, 34

O
Orchestrated Chaos, 142

P
Painting the Night Sky, 159
Panic, 106
Passion, 165
Peeling a Black Hole, 116
Playing in the Den, 74
Poison, 77
Pretend, 108
Promise, 30
Puddles, 41

R
Realisation, 6
Repulsion, 162
Resilience, 184

S
Safe, 148
Safe Keeping, 171
Salty Waters, 104
Secure, 163
Shaping Clouds, 42
Shiver, 153
Silence, 64
Silence Sounds Better with
    You, 44
Skyline, 156
Slowing Down, 175
Someone, Somewhere, 9
Song and Dance, 5
Speechless, 48
Stay with Me, 126
Staying for Nothing, 91
Staying to Leave, 104
Stopping Time, 163
Stranger, 6
Sweet End, 149

T
Taking the Punches, 152
The Act of Healing, 178
The Bitter End, 76

Index

The Boundary, 200
The Burning Question, 20
The Dark Wizard, 129
The Dead Walking, 102
The Dependant, 176
The First Light of Day, 21
The Garden, 186
The Greatest Feeling, 139
The Hero, 187
The Morning After, 121
The Plan of Breaking, 105
The Right One, 161
The Spider's Web, 119
The Way We Hurt, 63
The World Begins with You, 209
Three Hours, 123
Time, 65
Touching Love, 4
Toxic, 13
Translate, 19

U
Unchained, 179
Unconditional Love, 5
Unsighted Hope, 17

W
Wandering Eyes, 66
Warm Moments, 172
Wayward Thoughts, 127

Wellness, 198
What Does Progression Look Like, 50
What You Sea, 57
Why Not You, 184
Wilted Memories, 71
Without a Touch, 43
Writing Pain, 18

Y
You Hurt to Become Better, 175

www.ingramcontent.com/pod-product-compliance
Lightning Source LLC
Chambersburg PA
CBHW031532040426
42445CB00010B/497